ABRAHAM LINCOLN

PIVOTAL PRESIDENTS
PROFILES IN LEADERSHIP

ABRAHAM LINCOLN

Edited by Michael Anderson

Britannica
Educational Publishing
IN ASSOCIATION WITH

ROSEN
EDUCATIONAL SERVICES

Published in 2013 by Britannica Educational Publishing
(a trademark of Encyclopædia Britannica, Inc.) in association with Rosen Educational Services, LLC
29 East 21st Street, New York, NY 10010.

First Edition

Britannica Educational Publishing
J.E. Luebering: Director, Core Reference Group, Encyclopædia Britannica
Adam Augustyn: Assistant Manager, Encyclopædia Britannica

Anthony L. Green: Editor, Compton's by Britannica
Michael Anderson: Senior Editor, Compton's by Britannica
Andrea R. Field: Senior Editor, Compton's by Britannica
Sherman Hollar: Senior Editor, Compton's by Britannica

Marilyn L. Barton: Senior Coordinator, Production Control
Steven Bosco: Director, Editorial Technologies
Lisa S. Braucher: Senior Producer and Data Editor
Yvette Charboneau: Senior Copy Editor
Kathy Nakamura: Manager, Media Acquisition

Rosen Educational Services
Hope Lourie Killcoyne: Executive Editor
Nelson Sá: Art Director
Cindy Reiman: Photography Manager
Karen Huang: Photo Researcher
Brian Garvey: Designer, Cover Design
Introduction by Hope Lourie Killcoyne

Library of Congress Cataloging-in-Publication Data

Abraham Lincoln/edited by Michael Anderson.
    p. cm. — (Pivotal Presidents: Profiles in Leadership)
"In association with Britannica Educational Publishing, Rosen Educational Services."
Includes bibliographical references and index.
ISBN 978-1-61530-942-9 (library binding)
1. Lincoln, Abraham, 1809–1865—Juvenile literature. 2. Presidents—United States—Biography—
Juvenile literature. 3. United States—History—Civil War, 1861–1865—Juvenile literature. 4. United
States—Politics and government—1861–1865—Juvenile literature. I. Anderson, Michael, 1972–
E457.905.A293 2012
973.7092—dc23
[B]

                                                                                    2012020487

Manufactured in the United States of America

On the cover, page 3: Behind the portrait of Abraham Lincoln, the 16th president of the United States,
is an illustration depicting the Battle of Antietam, one of the bloodiest battles of the American Civil
War. It was on the heels of this Union victory that Lincoln issued what he called "the central act" of
his administration: the Emancipation Proclamation, which freed all slaves in Confederate states. *Stock
Montage/Archive Photos/Getty Images (Lincoln); Buyenlarge/Archive Photos/Getty Images (Antietam).*

Cover, pp. 1, 3 (flag) © iStockphoto.com/spxChrome; pp. 5, 12, 23, 39, 49, 70, 73, 76, 78 Fedrov Oleksiy/
Shutterstock.com

Table of Contents

A life-sized bronze statue of Abraham Lincoln stands in front of the entrance to the New York Historical Society. With the stovepipe hat, the statue is nearly 7 feet (2 meters) tall. *Hope Lourie Killcoyne*

For most Americans, conjuring a mental image of Abraham Lincoln is not that hard to do. The figure is tall. Lanky. There's the hat. The beard. The wry smile and the glint in the eye. Trying to visualize other presidents, though, is another story. Aside from recent leaders and some near-mythic early ones—Washington, Jefferson—very few strike the visual chord that Lincoln docs. (Admit it: try to picture Benjamin Harrison and the slate is blank.)

But Lincoln was not just a memorable face. Despite the fact that all told, Abe Lincoln, the 16th president of the United States of America, spent *less than a year* in school, he was a *brilliant* orator, issuing profound and precise sentiments that could not but command the attention of his listeners, be they sympathetic to his politics or not. Consider this prescient passage from one of his most famous speeches, delivered in 1858, two years before he was elected president and nearly three years before the start of the Civil War:

> *"A house divided against itself cannot stand.*
> *I believe this government cannot endure,*
> *permanently, half slave and half free. I*
> *do not expect the Union to be dissolved; I do*
> *not expect the house to fall; but I do expect*

it will cease to be divided. It will become all one thing, or all the other."

Or this line, delivered by then-President Lincoln to an Indiana regiment in March 1865, four years into the war:

"Whenever I hear anyone arguing for slavery, I feel a strong impulse to see it tried on him personally."

Perhaps it was the axe-wielding prowess Lincoln mastered in his early years that informed his way with words, allowing him to chop to the core of a complex issue, but he was a master at creating tight, pithy utterances. Perhaps the most memorable and extraordinary example of Lincoln's singular ability to find the essence of an occasion (or thought or emotion) was his 268-word Gettysburg Address in 1863. As president, Lincoln was asked to speak to those gathered at the dedication ceremony of the National Cemetery on the site of one of the Civil War's deadliest battles (nearly 8,000 soldiers died in the three-day struggle). His presence at the site was something of a postscript to the main speaker, Edward Everett, an erudite and esteemed orator of the day. Lincoln's speech began with the now indelible sentence:

> *"Four score and seven years ago our fathers brought forth on this continent a new nation, conceived in liberty and dedicated to the proposition that all men are created equal."*

Lincoln's speech took a mere three minutes; Everett's lasted two hours. It is a fairly safe bet that most Americans do not even remember that Everett spoke at Gettysburg on that day, but say those words from Lincoln's address, and they will know, if not whence it came, then at least who said it.

Lincoln's character is also well known. Honest. Hardworking. Humble. Intelligent. Thoughtfully decisive. He was not, however, always strictly serious, and his sense of humor is sometimes overlooked. Witness this line, uttered (and then recounted) by Lincoln in a dream of his in response to an observer commenting that he was a common-looking man:

> *"Common-looking people are the best in the world: that is the reason the Lord makes so many of them."*

What readers also may not know about Lincoln — and will learn in this book — is that he was a gifted wrestler. And that before becoming a lawyer, a member of the Illinois General Assembly, a representative of Illinois in the U.S. Congress, and ultimately one of the most pivotal presidents of the United States of America, he had held jobs as a rail splitter, a postmaster, a store clerk, a ferryboat pilot, and a surveyor. Many hats for the man famous for wearing the stovepipe hat. But as the multitalented and variously employed man from Kentucky once said:

"Whatever you are, be a good one."

CHAPTER 1

Early Life

The 16th president of the United States, Abraham Lincoln not only ranks among the greatest of all American statesmen; many historians also place him among the greatest men of all time. Lincoln came to the presidency at a time of extreme crisis, with the country at the brink of a civil war that threatened to split North from South. Combining his roles as statesman and commander in chief, Lincoln led the federal armies to victory and held the Union together. Along the way he brought about the end of slavery in the United States.

CHILDHOOD

Abraham Lincoln was born on Feb. 12, 1809, in a one-room log cabin on a farm near

Abraham Lincoln. *Library of Congress, Washington, D.C.*

Hodgenville, Ky. His parents were Thomas and Nancy Lincoln. He had an older sister, Sarah, and a younger brother, Thomas, who died in infancy. In 1811 Thomas Lincoln moved the family to a farm in the neighboring valley of Knob Creek. In later years Abraham Lincoln said that the Knob Creek farm was the first home he remembered and that he loved it.

One of Abraham Lincoln's boyhood homes was a log cabin at Knob Creek, in central Kentucky. The cabin was originally built in the early 19th century. *Wettach/Shostal Associates*

In December 1816 the family moved across the Ohio River to the backwoods of southwestern Indiana. The Lincolns settled on Little Pigeon Creek in Spencer County, about 16 miles (26 kilometers) from the Ohio River. Abe and Sarah helped their father build a "half-faced camp." This was a shed of poles and bark, with one side left open toward a roaring log fire.

While the rest of the family huddled in their lean-to through the freezing winter, Thomas and Abe worked every day building a log cabin. Abe was only eight years old but very large for his age, and he quickly learned to swing an ax. Once in a while the boy shot a wild turkey, for the family lived mostly on wild game, with a little corn. He never became much of a hunter, however, as he did not like to shoot to kill. With Sarah he picked berries, nuts, and wild fruits for the family and trudged a mile to a spring for water.

In 1818 Nancy Hanks Lincoln died of the frontier disease called milk sickness — that is, drinking milk from cows that had grazed on the toxic plant called white snakeroot. Sarah, only 11 years old, took over the cooking and cabin chores while Thomas and Abe cut timber to clear farmland.

Abe's "Angel Mother"

Abe and his sister, Sarah, quickly learned to love their stepmother, Sarah. She had a quiet way of getting things done. She cleaned up the cabin. She had Thomas make a wood floor and chairs and build a bed for the feather mattress she had brought from Kentucky. Abe and Sarah had never lived in a cabin so homelike. Thomas did better on the farm, too, and the children began to eat and dress better. In later years Abe said of his stepmother: "She was the best friend I ever had. . . . All that I am, I owe to my angel mother." Sarah Lincoln told people: "He was the best boy I ever saw. I never gave him a cross word in all my life. His mind and mine, what little I had, seemed to run together."

Sarah Bush Lincoln, née Johnston, Abraham Lincoln's stepmother. *Hulton Archive/Getty Images*

After a year the family was struggling without a wife and mother. Then Thomas rode back to Elizabethtown, Ky., and married a widow, Sarah Bush Johnston, whom he had known since childhood. He brought her and her three children to the log cabin in Indiana.

EDUCATION

Abe started school at a log schoolhouse when he was six years old. There he learned reading, writing, and arithmetic. He liked writing best of all. With all of the work to be done on the farm, Thomas did not make education a priority for his children. His wife, Sarah, however, encouraged Abe to study. She was not educated, but she saw how eager he was to learn.

Sarah made Thomas send 11-year-old Abe to school. There was no regular teacher. When someone came along who knew a little about a subject, that person might teach the boys and girls for a few weeks—usually in the winter when farmwork was slow. Whenever school was in session at Pigeon Creek, Abe hiked 4 miles (6.4 kilometers) each way. He did not mind this long, uncomfortable hike to and from school because he was glad to be learning. All subjects fascinated him.

Abe once said that, as a boy, he had gone to school "by littles"—a little now and a little then. In all, his schooling did not add up to a year, but he made up for it by reading. By the time Abe was 14, he would often read at night by the light of the log fire. His neighbors later recalled how he used to trudge for miles to borrow a book. The first books he read included the Bible, *Aesop's Fables*, Daniel Defoe's *Robinson Crusoe*, and Parson Weems's *The Life and Memorable Actions of George Washington*.

Abraham Lincoln as a young man reading a book as he leans against a felled tree, early 1800s. *George Eastman House/Archive Photos/Getty Images*

When he was 15 years old, Abe was so tall and strong that he often worked as a hired hand on other farms. Usually, while he plowed or split fence rails, he kept a borrowed book tucked in his shirt to read while he lunched or rested.

BOATMAN AND LAW "LISTENER"

After supper Abe often walked down the road to Gentryville and spent time at Gentry's general store. His humorous stories, sometimes told in dialect, made him popular there. He loved to imitate travelers and local characters and would throw back his head with a booming laugh. In his own speech he pronounced words as he had learned them on the Kentucky frontier, such as "cheer" for "chair" and "git" for "get."

Between farm chores Abe helped to run a ferry across the Ohio River to Kentucky. When he was 18, he built his own scow and rowed passengers over the shallows to steamboats out in the river.

Always he kept teaching himself new things. He became interested in law. Borrowing a book on the laws of Indiana, he

A young Abraham Lincoln ferrying passengers across the Ohio River at one of his first jobs. *Kean Collection/Archive Photos/Getty Images*

studied it long into the night. He strode miles to the nearest courthouse to hear lawyers try cases. He even crossed into Kentucky to listen in court. Every visit taught him more about the ways of lawyers and furnished

This illustration, by Joseph Boggs Beale, shows Abraham Lincoln *(at left, in blue pants)* **watching a slave auction in New Orleans, Louisiana.** *George Eastman House/Archive Photos/Getty Images*

him with new stories. Throughout his later life as a lawyer, politician, and statesman, he shrewdly drew on this rich fund of stories to make a legal point or to win audiences.

When Abe was 19, he got his first chance to see something of the larger world. James Gentry, the owner of the general store, hired him to take a flatboat of cargo down the Mississippi River to New Orleans, La., then a wealthy city of some 40,000 people.

In New Orleans Abe saw for the first time an auction of slaves. At that time slavery was lawful in the United States south of the Ohio River. The tall, thoughtful young man winced at the sight of slaves in chains being marched off to plantations. Later he said, "Slavery was a continual torment to me."

CHAPTER 2

Lincoln in Illinois

Back from New Orleans, Lincoln clerked part-time at Gentry's store and helped his father get ready to move to Illinois. The Indiana farm had not been a success. Through the winter the men built wagons and chests and made yokes and harnesses. In March 1830 the family started their 200-mile (320-kilometer) trek. They settled on the Sangamon River, some 10 miles (16 kilometers) southwest of Decatur, Ill.

At the age of 21 Lincoln was about to begin life on his own. Six feet four inches tall, he was lanky but muscular and physically powerful. He was especially noted for the skill and strength with which he could wield an ax. He helped to clear and fence his father's new farm and then, with a cousin, split 3,000

A painting from about 1830 shows Abraham Lincoln cutting logs, an occupation that would later earn him the nickname of "rail-splitter."
MPI/Archive Photos/Getty Images

rails to fence some neighbors' land. His feats with an ax on the Illinois prairie led his political supporters to call him, later in life, the "rail-splitter."

ARRIVAL IN NEW SALEM

After a winter of cold and illness Thomas Lincoln again moved, about 100 miles (160 kilometers) southeast into Coles County. This time Abe did not go. He was determined to make his own way. After a second voyage to New Orleans as a flatboatman, Lincoln settled in New Salem, Ill., a village of about 25 families on the Sangamon River, about 20 miles (32 kilometers) northwest of Springfield. Here he lived for six years, from 1831 to 1837. For $15 a month and a sleeping room in the back, he tended a store and a gristmill.

Tales sprang up fast about Lincoln in the New Salem days. People spoke about his strict honesty. Some told how he once walked 6 miles (10 kilometers) to give back a few pennies to a woman who had overpaid for dry goods. Whenever settlers bought furs, or an oxen yoke, guns, tea, or salt, they knew they

Abraham Lincoln working behind the counter at the general store in New Salem, Ill., 1830s. *Kean Collection/Archive Photos/ Getty Images*

would get their money's worth from "honest Abe." Lincoln earned respect of another kind for his physical prowess. Along with his skills as a rail-splitter, he impressed the townspeople with his wrestling ability. In matches with powerful opponents, Lincoln often simply tossed them over his head.

Lincoln and the Black Hawk War

When the Black Hawk War broke out in April 1832, Lincoln enlisted as a volunteer. In this war a group of Sauk and Fox Indians led by Black Hawk defiantly crossed from Iowa into Illinois in an attempt to reclaim land that the government had taken from them. Lincoln was elected captain of a rifle company. The honor pleased him, but he knew nothing about military life.

When Lincoln's term of enlistment ended in 30 days, he re-enlisted as a private. In all he served three months, but he never fought in a battle. Afterward he joked that he had seen no "live, fighting Indians" during the war but had had "a good many bloody struggles with the mosquitoes." Still, his army experience—being on long marches and in rough camps—taught him sympathy for soldiers' hardships in the field. In later life, when he was commander in chief in the Civil War, he treated soldiers' failings with great understanding.

A VARIETY OF OCCUPATIONS

Just before the outbreak of the Black Hawk War, Lincoln had decided to run for the Illinois legislature, called the General Assembly. After his war service he again started his campaign. In a circular he sent out to voters, he wrote: "I was born and have remained in the most humble walks of life." He did not carry the district, but his local popularity gave him nearly every vote in New Salem.

Meanwhile the New Salem store failed. Lincoln was out of work. He thought of learning to be a blacksmith, but another New Salem store was put up for sale. Lincoln, with William Berry as partner, bought it on credit. Neither one, however, was much interested in tending to business. Lincoln preferred to visit with the few customers or to read. After several months Berry died, leaving Lincoln more than $1,000 in debt. Eventually he paid back every cent, but it took him years.

Failing as a storekeeper, Lincoln was again struggling. In May 1833 his friends got him appointed postmaster of New Salem. The job paid only about $50 a year, but it took

The ever-studious Abe Lincoln, axe in one hand and book in another, *c.* 1835. *Stock Montage/Archive Photos/Getty Images*

little of his time and gave him the chance to read all the incoming newspapers for free. He read every issue and was particularly interested in the political news. To earn his board and lodging, he also split rails and worked as a mill hand and hired man. In every spare moment he read or made political talks.

In the autumn of 1833 Lincoln gladly took an appointment as deputy county surveyor. To learn the work, he plunged into books on surveying and mathematics. By studying all day, and sometimes all night, he learned surveying in six weeks. As he rode about the county, laying out roads and towns, he lived with different families and made new friends.

STATE LEGISLATURE

In 1834 Lincoln's old friends in New Salem and his new friends throughout Sangamon County elected him to the Illinois General Assembly. They reelected him in 1836, 1838, and 1840. Before his first term began in November 1834, he borrowed $200 to pay the most pressing of his debts and to buy a suit for his new work.

When Lincoln entered politics, Andrew Jackson was president. Lincoln shared the sympathies that Jackson and his supporters had for the common people. He disagreed, though, with the Jacksonian view that the government should not be involved in economic enterprise. "The legitimate object of government," he was later to say, "is to do for a community of people whatever they need to have done, but cannot do at all, or cannot do so well, for themselves, in their separate and individual capacities."

Among the prominent politicians of the time, Lincoln most admired Henry Clay and Daniel Webster. Clay and Webster supported using the powers of the federal government to encourage business and develop the country's resources by means of a national bank, a protective tariff, and a program of transportation improvements. In Lincoln's view, Illinois and the West as a whole desperately needed such aid for economic development. From the start, he associated himself with the party of Clay and Webster, the Whigs.

Lincoln soon became popular in the legislature. One representative said that Lincoln was "raw-boned . . . ungraceful . . . almost uncouth . . . and yet there was a magnetism about the man that made him a universal favorite." By the time he started his second term, he was a skilled politician and a leader of the Whig Party in Illinois. A fellow Whig declared: "We followed his lead; but he followed nobody's lead. . . . He was poverty itself, but independent."

As a legislator Lincoln devoted himself to a huge project for constructing a network of railroads, highways, and canals. Whigs and Democrats joined in passing a bill for the project, but a business depression halted the plans.

Lincoln also showed that, though he opposed slavery, he was no abolitionist—that is, he did not want to abolish, or end, the practice. In 1837 the legislature introduced resolutions condemning abolitionist societies and defending slavery in the Southern states as "sacred" by virtue of the federal Constitution. Lincoln refused to vote for the resolutions. Together with a fellow member, he drew up a protest that declared that slavery was "founded on both injustice and bad policy." The protest also stated, however, that "the promulgation of abolition doctrines tends rather to increase than to abate its evils."

PRAIRIE LAWYER

Encouraged by friends in the legislature, Lincoln decided to become a lawyer. Between legislative terms he borrowed law books to study. He took some time from his studying to serve as New Salem's postmaster and did some surveying work. On Sept. 9, 1836, he received his law license.

In 1837 Lincoln led the drive to have the state capital transferred from Vandalia to Springfield. The legislature did not meet there until 1839, but in April 1837 Lincoln left New Salem to make his home in Springfield. The thriving town offered many more opportunities for a lawyer than New Salem did.

Within a few years of his move to Springfield, Lincoln had made a reputation for himself as a lawyer. He was earning $1,200 to $1,500 a year, at a time when the state governor received a salary of $1,200. He had to work hard. To keep himself busy, he found it necessary not only to practice in the capital but also to follow the court as it made the rounds of its judicial district, or circuit. Each spring and fall he set out by horseback or buggy to travel hundreds of miles over the thinly settled prairie, from one little county seat to another. He was away from home nearly six months of each year. Most of the cases were petty and the fees small.

Still, Lincoln enjoyed riding the circuit. He loved the easy comradeship of fellow lawyers staying in country inns and delighted in the sharp give-and-take in court. Wherever he went, he could make the jury and courtroom weep or break down in laughter. Even more important to his success was his reputation for honesty. Honest Abe would not take a case unless he believed in the client's innocence or rights.

PRIVATE LIFE

Once established as a lawyer in Springfield, Lincoln took part in the busy social life of the city. One of the society belles was a young woman named Mary Todd. She had come from her home in Lexington, Ky., to live with her sister and brother-in-law, son of the governor of Illinois. At that time Mary was 21 years old. Lincoln first met her in the winter of 1839 at a dance.

Soon Lincoln was spending every free moment with Mary Todd, who was high spirited, quick witted, and unusually well educated. They both loved literature and poetry, especially Shakespeare and Robert Burns. Lincoln delighted in reciting passages from memory. He was also pleased that Mary took an interest in politics.

A daguerreotype of Mary Todd Lincoln, c. 1846. *Library of Congress Prints and Photographs Division*

Stephen Douglas. *Library of Congress, Washington, D.C.*

Mary Todd was also being courted by Stephen Douglas, a prominent lawyer, with whom Lincoln was later to debate dramatically. Her wealthy, aristocratic family was opposed to Lincoln, whom they considered to be "uncouth, full of rough edges." Mary, as always, knew exactly what she wanted. By the spring she was devoted to Lincoln, and the two became engaged.

After a series of temperamental clashes between them, Mary Todd, the Kentucky belle, and Abraham Lincoln, the country lawyer, married on Nov. 4, 1842. They were living in one room at the Globe Tavern in Springfield when their first child, Robert

Todd, was born in 1843. During the next year Lincoln bought a house on the edge of town. There Edward, William, and Thomas (Tad) were born in 1846, 1850, and 1853, respectively. Robert Todd was the only one of the children to survive to adulthood, though Lincoln's favorite, Tad, outlived his father.

The Lincolns' home life was often stormy. Both of them were at fault. An extremely sensitive woman who was afflicted with migraine headaches, Mary frequently gave way to rages of uncontrollable temper. Sometimes they may have been justified, for Lincoln had

This painting shows the Lincoln family in the White House in 1862, after the death of Willie. Tad sits at Lincoln's knee. Robert, the eldest son, stands between his father and mother. *Library of Congress, Washington, D.C.*

trying habits. Most arose from his enormous power of concentration. When he became interested in a book or a problem, he forgot everything else. Lincoln went to bed at all hours and got up at all hours. For no apparent reason he sank into black, silent moods for hours, and sometimes days, at a time. Nevertheless, the Lincolns shared a devotion to their sons, enjoyed one another's company, and missed each other when apart.

CHAPTER 3

National Politics

In 1847 Lincoln went to Washington, D.C., as a representative from Illinois. The Mexican War was on, and Lincoln opposed it. His antiwar speeches displeased his political supporters. He knew they would not reelect him.

At the end of his term in 1849 he returned to Springfield. He sought an appointment as commissioner in the General Land Office in Washington, but he failed to get it. Later that year he was offered the governorship of the Oregon Territory. He refused, convinced that he was now a failure in politics.

RETURN TO LAW

For about five years Lincoln took little part in politics. Resuming his law practice, he again

One of the earliest known photographs of Lincoln was taken in Springfield, Ill., in 1846, when he was 37 years old. He did not grow his beard until 1861. *Library of Congress, Washington, D.C.*

rode the circuit. The coming of the railroads, especially after 1850, made travel easier and his practice more lucrative.

Lincoln served as a lobbyist for the Illinois Central Railroad, assisting it in getting a charter from the state in 1851. Thereafter he worked as a regular attorney for the railroad. Lincoln also handled cases for other railroads and for banks, insurance companies, and mercantile and manufacturing firms. One of his finest performances before the bar came in a case involving the Rock Island Bridge. The first bridge to span the Mississippi River, it was built to ease railroad transportation. Steamboat companies opposed the bridge on the grounds that it interfered with river shipping. Representing the railroads, Lincoln saved the bridge and,

Lincoln's Most Famous Case

Lincoln's law practice included a number of criminal trials. Perhaps his most famous case was his defense of Duff Armstrong, an acquaintance of his who was accused of murder. A witness said he had seen Duff bludgeon and kill a man by the light of the Moon. Lincoln opened an almanac, which recorded that the Moon on that night had set long before the scuffle. He argued that the night had been too dark for the witness to have seen anything clearly. With a sincere and moving appeal, he won an acquittal.

in a broader sense, affirmed the right of rail-roads to cross rivers.

BACK TO POLITICS

The threat of slavery being extended brought Lincoln back into politics in 1854. He did not suggest interfering with slavery in states where it was already lawful. The Kansas-Nebraska Act of 1854, however, enabled the people of each new territory to vote on whether the territory would be slave or free, thus threatening to extend slavery. Lincoln gave a series of speeches protesting the act.

In 1856 he helped to organize the Illinois branch of the new Republican Party, a political party formed by people who wanted to stop the spread of slavery. He became the leading Republican in Illinois. When the Republicans nominated John C. Frémont for the presidency of the United States, Lincoln received 110 votes for nomination as vice president. This brought Lincoln to the attention of the country.

The Republicans lost the presidential election, but in 1858 Lincoln won the Republican nomination for senator from

Illinois. Addressing the state convention in Springfield, he gave the first of his memorable speeches. His hands tensely gripping the speaker's stand, he declared slowly and firmly: "A house divided against itself cannot stand. I believe this government cannot endure permanently, half slave and half free. I do not expect the Union to be dissolved—I do not expect the house to fall—but I do

Life-sized bronze statues of Stephen A. Douglas *(left)* and Abraham Lincoln at the site of their 1858 debate in Alton, Ill. © *Melinda Leonard*

expect it will cease to be divided. It will become all one thing, or all the other."

Lincoln's opponent in the senatorial election was Stephen A. Douglas, a Democrat and Lincoln's political (and former romantic) rival. Douglas was running for reelection and had supported the Kansas-Nebraska Act. Lincoln challenged him to a series of debates on the slavery issue. Although he overwhelmed Douglas in the debates, Lincoln lost the election. The outcome did not surprise him, but it depressed him deeply. The debates, however, had enlarged the public interest in Lincoln and began earning him a national reputation.

Abraham Lincoln, 1860. *Library of Congress Prints and Photographs Division*

Realizing his countrywide fame, Lincoln's friends sought the Republican nomination for president for him in 1860. He himself worked tirelessly to win support. He now knew what he wanted—to be president of the United States in its time of crisis. He was determined to preserve the Union. At the Republican National Convention in Chicago, he was nominated on the third ballot.

CAMPAIGN AND ELECTION

The Democratic Party was split, with the North nominating Stephen A. Douglas and the South choosing John C. Breckinridge. Throughout the furious campaign Lincoln stayed quietly in Springfield, directing party leaders from a makeshift office in the Capitol. He even carried his own mail back and forth from the post office. To avoid stirring up controversy and perhaps splitting the Republicans, he did not make a single political speech.

The strategy worked. On Nov. 6, 1860, Lincoln was elected 16th president of the United States. He had 1,866,452 votes, Douglas had 1,380,202, and Breckinridge, 847,953. A fourth candidate, John Bell of the

This photograph was taken during Lincoln's "stay-at-home" presidential campaign in 1860. He bought the house in 1843, for $1,500, then added the second story. *Encyclopædia Britannica, Inc.*

Constitutional Union Party, received 590,901 votes. Although Lincoln's total represented only 40 percent of the popular vote, he won by a large margin in the electoral college. He received no votes from the Deep South. Lincoln was the first Republican to become president. His vice president was Hannibal Hamlin of Maine.

Alarm spread through the Southern states. They thought a Republican president would not respect their rights or property. They felt that secession was their only hope. Secession began on Dec. 20, 1860, when South Carolina withdrew from the Union. Six more Southern states seceded before Lincoln took office. They formed their own government, calling themselves the Confederate States of America.

As the time of Lincoln's inauguration approached, threats to kill him increased. They failed to frighten him, but no one was

An American flag banner promotes Lincoln for the presidency in 1860. *Library of Congress Prints and Photographs Division*

more aware of the danger of his position in a time of crisis. Saying farewell to friends at the Springfield railway station, he said prophetically: "I now leave, not knowing when, or whether ever, I may return, with a task before me greater than that which rested on Washington."

CHAPTER 4

Presidency

In his inaugural address, delivered on March 4, 1861, Lincoln assured the South that he would respect its rights, that there was no need for war. He said: "I have no

The inauguration of Abraham Lincoln as U.S. president, Washington, D.C., March 4, 1861. *Library of Congress Prints and Photographs Division*

purpose . . . to interfere with the institution of slavery in states where it exists. . . . In your hands, my dissatisfied fellow countrymen, and not in mine, is the momentous issue of civil war. . . . We must not be enemies."

Nevertheless, less than six weeks later, on April 12, 1861, the Civil War began when Confederate forces fired on U.S. troops at Fort Sumter. The war would completely consume Lincoln's administration. The president shouldered the giant task of bringing the rebel states back into the national family and preserving the Union.

LEADERSHIP IN WARTIME

Lincoln was a strong president. At first his deliberate thinking and extraordinary patience deceived his Cabinet into thinking him uncertain. Profiting by his experience as a lawyer, he looked at every side of a question before deciding on an answer. When Lincoln reached a decision, he was firm. His Cabinet soon discovered this. Once every Cabinet member opposed Lincoln's plan. He smiled, said "Aye" for his own vote, and calmly announced, "The aye has it." Still, Lincoln remained flexible and open to new ideas. If one action or decision

President Abraham Lincoln *(seated center)* and his Cabinet, with Lieut. Gen. Winfield Scott, are depicted in the council chamber at the White House. *Library of Congress, Washington, D.C.*

proved unsatisfactory in practice, he was willing to experiment with another.

After the firing on Fort Sumter, Lincoln called upon the state governors for troops (Virginia and three other states of the upper South responded by joining the Confederacy). He then proclaimed a blockade of the Southern ports. These were the first important decisions of Lincoln as commander in chief of the Army and Navy. But he still needed a strategic plan and a command system for carrying it out.

Early in the war Lincoln had trouble finding capable generals to lead the Union forces. As with his Cabinet, he gave Gen. George B. McClellan and others every chance to prove themselves. When McClellan continued to delay attacking the Confederate forces, Lincoln said wryly, "He's got the slows." He kept urging McClellan to advance. Instead, McClellan ignored Lincoln.

Soon Lincoln felt that he himself must take action. He read all he could on military science and made frequent inspection trips of forces in the field. Sometimes he took Mary Lincoln and his youngest son, Tad, with him to help boost the morale of the troops. Until he found competent generals, he directed much of the strategy for the Army and the Navy.

Eventually Lincoln looked to the West for a top general. He admired the Vicksburg Campaign of Ulysses S. Grant in Mississippi, which had cut the Confederacy in two. In March 1864 Lincoln promoted Grant to lieutenant general and gave him command of all the federal armies. At last Lincoln had found a man who could helm the large-scale, coordinated offensive that he had in mind. Grant was only a member, though an important one, of a top-command structure that Lincoln had devised.

794£

President Abraham Lincoln and Gen. George B. McClellan in the general's tent, Antietam, Md., Oct. 3, 1862. Photograph by Alexander Gardner. *Library of Congress Prints and Photographs Division*

The command also included Secretary of War Edwin M. Stanton and Chief of Staff Henry W. Halleck. Overseeing everything was Lincoln himself, as commander in chief.

Lincoln made mistakes in his conduct of the war. On the whole, however, he was a successful commander in chief. His effectiveness as a wartime leader increased year by year. His achievement is all the more remarkable in view of his lack of training and experience in warfare.

Ulysses S. Grant, in the uniform of lieutenant-general. In March 1864, during the Civil War, President Lincoln promoted Grant to this rank and placed him in command of all Union armies. Later, from 1869 to 1877, Grant served as the 18th president of the United States. *Universal Images Group/Getty Images*

C.W. Reed's cartoon *Lincoln's Midnight Think* depicting President Abraham Lincoln agonizing over the conduct of the Civil War. *Library of Congress, Washington, D.C.*

EMANCIPATION PROCLAMATION

Lincoln was deeply devoted to the cause of personal freedom. Yet, as president, he was at first reluctant to adopt an abolitionist policy. There were several reasons for his hesitancy. He had been elected on a platform pledging no interference with slavery. He was concerned about the possible difficulties of incorporating nearly 4 million African Americans, once they had been freed, into the country's social and political life.

Above all, Lincoln felt that he must hold the border slave states in the Union. He feared that an abolitionist program might push them toward the Confederacy. In August 1862 he wrote: "My paramount object in this struggle is to save the Union, and it is not either to save or to destroy slavery. If I could save the Union without freeing any slave, I would do it; and if I could save it by freeing all the slaves I would do it; and if I could save it by freeing some and leaving others alone, I would also do that."

Yet Lincoln knew that the slavery question must be settled if the United States, founded on the principles of liberty and equal rights for all, were to survive as a country. He realized that the Union must be preserved, as a free nation, if democratic government was to succeed in the world.

As antislavery sentiment rose, Lincoln worked out a plan to emancipate, or free, the slaves. According to his proposal, the slaves were to be freed by the states. The emancipation process was to be gradual. The slaveholders were to be compensated, with the federal government sharing the cost. The newly freed blacks were to be colonized outside the United States. Congress approved the plan, but the border slave states rejected it. In addition, few African American leaders wanted to see their people sent abroad.

Lincoln did not abandon hope for the veventual success of his gradual plan. Still, he took quite a different step by drawing up another proposal. His Cabinet approved issuing the new proclamation after the next Union victory. The summer of 1862 passed with no victory. Then, on September 17, Union forces stopped the advancing Confederate armies at Antietam, Md.

On Sept. 22, 1862, Lincoln put forth his preliminary proclamation. It promised freedom for slaves in any Confederate state that did not return to the Union that year. When

By the President of the United States of America:

A Proclamation.

Whereas, on the twenty-second day of September, in the year of our Lord one thousand eight hundred and sixty-two, a proclamation was issued by the President of the United States, containing, among other things, the following, to wit:

"That on the first day of January, in the "year of our Lord one thousand eight hundred "and sixty-three, all persons held as slaves within "any State or designated part of a State, the people "whereof shall then be in rebellion against the "United States, shall be then, thenceforward, and "forever free; and the Executive Government of the "United States, including the military and naval "authority thereof, will recognize and maintain "the freedom of such persons, and will do no act "or acts to repress such persons, or any of them, "in any efforts they may make for their actual

Abraham Lincoln called the Emancipation Proclamation "the central act of my administration, and the greatest event of the 19th century." *AFP/Getty Images*

the South ignored him, he issued the final Emancipation Proclamation on Jan. 1, 1863. It was a landmark moment. It transformed the war from a struggle to preserve the Union into a crusade for human freedom.

Lincoln justified the Emancipation Proclamation as an exercise of the president's war powers. Yet even he doubted whether it fell within his authority under the Constitution. After the war, the slaves freed by the proclamation could have possibly been enslaved again had nothing else been done to confirm their freedom. But something else was done. In 1865 Lincoln urged Congress to approve the 13th Amendment to the Constitution, which outlawed slavery in the United States.

WARTIME POLITICS

To win the war, Lincoln had to have politicians and the public behind him. Therefore he gave much of his time and attention to politics, trying to attract the support of as many people as possible. Fortunately for the Union cause, Lincoln was a president with rare political skill. He had the knack of appealing to fellow politicians and talking to them in their own language. He had a talent

Gettysburg Address

In July 1863 the Union armies turned back the Confederate forces at Gettysburg, Pa. This was the only battle on Northern soil.

On Nov. 19, 1863, the battlefield was dedicated as a national cemetery. The chief speaker was Edward Everett, a noted orator. As an afterthought, Lincoln was invited "to make a few appropriate remarks." He worked and reworked his speech, seeking to make it as perfect as possible.

The crowd listened for two hours to Everett's extravagant oratory. Lincoln then rose slowly, put on his glasses, glanced at a slip of paper, and then spoke gravely in his clear, high-pitched voice. In a little less than three minutes he finished his Gettysburg Address, ending with the words:

> *...that from these honored dead we take increased devotion to that cause for which they gave the last full measure of devotion—that we here highly resolve that these dead shall not have died in vain—that this nation, under God, shall have a new birth of freedom—and that government of the people, by the people, for the people, shall not perish from the Earth.*

Lincoln thought the speech a failure, as did most of the newspapers. Only a few recognized it as one of the noblest speeches ever made. Everett wrote to him: "I should be glad if I could flatter myself that I came as near the central idea of the occasion in two hours as you did in two minutes."

The dedication ceremony for the National Cemetery at Gettysburg Battlefield was held in November 1863. Abraham Lincoln, hatless, is seated left of center. *Library of Congress, Washington, D.C.*

for smoothing over personal differences and holding the loyalty of politicians who disagreed with one another.

Opposition to Lincoln and war remained strong among Democrats in the North. A few "peace Democrats" even collaborated with the enemy. In dealing with people suspected of treason, Lincoln at times authorized his generals to make arbitrary arrests. He let his generals suspend several newspapers, though only for short periods. He believed that he had to allow the temporary sacrifice of some liberties guaranteed by the Constitution in order to maintain the Union and thus preserve the Constitution as a whole.

Considering the dangers of the time, Lincoln was quite liberal in his treatment of political opponents and the press. He was by no means the dictator critics often accused him of being. Nevertheless, his suspension of some civil liberties disturbed Democrats, Republicans, and even members of his own Cabinet.

Within the Republican Party, Lincoln faced divisions and personal rivalries that caused him as much trouble as did the Democrats. He and most other party members agreed fairly well upon their main economic aims. With his approval, the Republicans put into

Abraham Lincoln, photograph by Mathew Brady, 1864. *Library of Congress Prints and Photographs Division*

law the essential parts of the program he had advocated from his early Whig days. These included a protective tariff, a national banking system, and federal aid for internal improvements, in particular for the construction of a railroad to the Pacific coast. The Republicans disagreed among themselves, however, on many matters regarding the conduct and purposes of the war.

The big issue was the "reconstruction" of the South. As Southern states were retaken by the federal armies, the president and Congress put forth plans for bringing them back into the Union. Late in 1863 Lincoln proposed his "ten percent plan." It stated that a state government could be reestablished when 10 percent of the state's voters had taken an oath of loyalty to the United States. Some Republicans, called Radicals, rejected Lincoln's proposal. They thought he was being too easy on the rebel states. The Radical Republicans passed a stricter bill, which the president vetoed.

REELECTION AND DEATH

The Republicans nominated Lincoln for reelection in 1864. As in 1860, Lincoln was the chief strategist of his own campaign. He took a hand in the management of the Republican Speakers' Bureau and advised state committees on campaign tactics. He also did his best to enable as many soldiers and sailors as possible to vote.

By the time of the election in November 1864, however, Lincoln was nearly exhausted by the burden of the war and grief at the

The Union Christmas Dinner, published in *Harper's Weekly* in 1864, depicts President Lincoln's invitation to the South to rejoin the Union on an equal basis with the other states. *Library of Congress, Washington, D.C.*

death of his son Willie in the White House. Wherever he turned, he read or heard criticism of himself and his generals. He prepared a memorandum for his Cabinet, forecasting his defeat in the coming election. The people, however, at last rallied to him and reelected him, with Andrew Johnson as vice president. Little more than a month later, on April 9, 1865, Gen. Robert E. Lee surrendered his Confederate army to Gen. Ulysses S. Grant. On April 11 the Stars and Stripes

The assassination of President Lincoln at Ford's Theatre in Washington, D.C., on April 14, 1865, is depicted in a lithograph by Currier and Ives. *Library of Congress, Washington, D.C. (digital file no. 3b49830u)*

of the United States were raised over Fort Sumter, where the war had begun.

To celebrate the end of the war, Lincoln took Mary and two guests to Ford's Theatre on the night of April 14. During the third act of the play, *Our American Cousin*, John Wilkes Booth, a young actor who was pro-slavery and a Confederate sympathizer, crept into the presidential box and shot Lincoln in the head. Booth then leapt onto the stage, and, brandishing a dagger, he escaped. He was shot and killed on April 26 in a Virginia tobacco barn when soldiers and detectives surrounded and set fire to it.

Soldiers carried the unconscious president across the street to the nearest residence, a boardinghouse. There he died at 7:22 in the morning, never having regained consciousness. It was April 15, 1865 — 28 years to the day since he had left New Salem. As the Great Emancipator died, Secretary of War Stanton said softly, "Now he belongs to the ages." A funeral train carried the president's body back home to Springfield, Ill., where he lies buried in Oak Ridge Cemetery. The Lincoln Memorial in Washington, D.C., was dedicated to him in 1922.

IN THIS TEMPLE
AS IN THE HEARTS OF THE PEOPLE
FOR WHOM HE SAVED THE UNION
THE MEMORY OF ABRAHAM LINCOLN
IS ENSHRINED FOREVER

Statue of Abraham Lincoln at the Lincoln Memorial, Washington, D.C. *Jarno Gonzalez Zarraonandia/Shutterstock.com*

CONCLUSION

Lincoln has become a myth as well as a man. Apart from his historical role as savior of the Union and the Great Emancipator of the slaves, he has been celebrated for his remarkable life story and his fundamental humanity. Born in a log cabin on the frontier, Lincoln made his own way in life to rise to the country's highest office. He did so while remaining a firm idealist who would not be swayed from the right course of action, a man of kindly and brave patience, and a believer in what he called the "family of man."

Lincoln's legacy is complex, however. In his own time, many Southerners believed him to be the destroyer of their liberty and their way of life. Today, some conservative historians continue to criticize Lincoln for using the power of the national government to trample states' rights. In Lincoln's view, though, the Union had to be preserved at all costs. It was worth saving not only for its own sake but also because it embodied an ideal, the ideal of self-government. His passion as a spokesman for democracy is a key element of Lincoln's unique and enduring appeal—both for his fellow countrymen and also for people throughout the world.

Glossary

abolitionism Principles or measures fostering the abolition (end) of slavery.

almanac Publication containing astronomical and meteorological data for a given year and often including an assortment of other information.

blockade Isolation by a warring nation of an enemy area (as a harbor) by troops or warships to prevent passage of persons or supplies; a restrictive measure designed to obstruct the commerce and communications of a military foe.

bludgeon To hit with heavy impact.

board Daily meals often provided as payment for services.

buggy Light one-horse carriage (made with two wheels in England and with four wheels in the United States).

daguerreotype Early photograph produced on a silver or a silver-covered copper plate.

dialect Regional variety of language, the features of which—vocabulary, grammar, and pronunciation—distinguish it from other regional varieties.

dry goods Textiles, ready-to-wear clothing, and notions (as opposed to other shop-bought items, such as hardware and groceries).

flatboat Boat with a flat bottom and square ends used for transportation of bulky freight, especially in shallow waters.

gristmill Mill for grinding grain.

memorandum Informal written note.

mercantile Of or relating to merchants (that is, buyers and sellers of commodities for profit).

mill hand One who works in a building where grain is ground into flour.

promulgate Openly declare; proclaim.

Radical Republican During and after the American Civil War, a member of the Republican Party committed to emancipation of the slaves and later to the equal treatment of the freed blacks.

resolution Formal expression of opinion, will, or intent voted by an official body or assembled group; a declaration submitted to an assembly for adoption.

scow Large flat-bottomed boat with broad square ends used chiefly (but not exclusively) for transporting bulk material (such as ore, sand, or refuse).

secession Formal withdrawal from an organization.

shallows Shallow place or area in a body of water.

surveyor One whose occupation is surveying (that is, inspecting, examining, and reporting on a specified portion of Earth's surface).

tariff Tax imposed by a government on imported (or, in some countries, exported) goods. Tariffs are also known as duties or customs.

try To examine or investigate in a court of law.

Whig Member or supporter of an American political party formed in 1834 to oppose President Andrew Jackson and the Jacksonian Democrats. Associated chiefly with manufacturing, commercial, and financial interests, the Whig Party was succeeded by the Republican Party in about 1854.

yoke Wooden bar or frame by which two draft animals (such as oxen) are joined at the heads or necks for working together.

For More Information

Abraham Lincoln Presidential Library
112 North Sixth Street
Springfield, IL 62701
(217) 558-8844
Web site: http://www.alplm.org
Committed to promoting interest in the
life of Abraham Lincoln as well as the
history of Illinois, the Abraham Lincoln
Presidential Library is a research library
with programs, exhibits, and documents available to the public. Its vast
collection includes photographs, family
possessions, and letters from Lincoln's
correspondence.

Abraham Lincoln Presidential Museum
212 North Sixth Street
Springfield, IL 62701
(217) 782-5764
Web site: http://www.alplm.org

The Abraham Lincoln Presidential Museum has numerous exhibits dedicated to the life of Lincoln. Included are actual artifacts and images as well as scenes from Lincoln's life featuring life-sized figures. Plays and performances dramatize events of Lincoln's time.

Ford's Theatre
511 Tenth Street NW
Washington, DC 20004
(202) 638-2941
Web site: http://www.fordstheatre.org
In addition to the variety of performances it offers, Ford's Theatre, the site of Abraham Lincoln's assassination, has a museum and Center for Education and Leadership with exhibits and artifacts related to Lincoln's presidency.

National Civil War Museum
One Lincoln Circle at Reservoir Park
Harrisburg, PA 17103
(717) 260-1861
Web site: http://www.nationalcivilwarmuseum
.org
The National Civil War Museum is committed to preserving artifacts, documents, photographs, and more from the Civil

War era and to presenting an unbiased view of the conflict to visitors through its various exhibits.

President Lincoln's Cottage
AFRH-W Box 1315
3700 North Capitol Street NW
Washington, DC 20011
(202) 829-0436
Web site: http://www.lincolncottage.org
President Lincoln's Cottage, where Abraham Lincoln resided for a quarter of his presidency and where he held a number of important meetings, offers tours and exhibits, highlighting some of the most significant decisions Lincoln made during the Civil War and his presidency.

WEB SITES

Due to the changing nature of Internet links, Rosen Educational Services has developed an online list of Web sites related to the subject of this book. This site is updated regularly. Please use this link to access the list:

www.rosenlinks.com/pppl/abelin

For Further Reading

Bishop, Jim. *The Day Lincoln Was Shot* (Greenwich House, 1984; orig. pub. 1955).

Fleming, Candace. *The Lincolns: A Scrapbook Look at Abraham and Mary* (Schwartz & Wade, 2008).

Freedman, Russell. *Lincoln: A Photobiography* (Clarion, 1987).

Holzer, Harold, and Shenk, J.W., eds. *In Lincoln's Hand: His Original Manuscripts* (Bantam Dell, 2009).

Lincoln, Abraham. *The Wit and Wisdom of Abraham Lincoln*, ed. by Alex Ayres (Meridian, 1992).

Marrin, Albert. *Commander in Chief: Abraham Lincoln and the Civil War* (Dutton Children's Books, 2003).

McPherson, J.M. *Abraham Lincoln* (Oxford Univ. Press, 2009).

Oates, S.B. *With Malice Toward None: The Life of Abraham Lincoln* (American Political Biography Press, 2002; orig. pub. 1977).

Sandburg, Carl. *Abraham Lincoln: The Prairie Years and the War Years* (Sterling, 2007; orig. pub. 1954).

Shenk, J.W. *Lincoln's Melancholy: How Depression Challenged a President and Fueled His Greatness* (Houghton, 2006).

Simon, Paul. *Lincoln's Preparation for Greatness: The Illinois Legislative Years* (Univ. of Ill. Press, 1989; orig. pub. 1965).

Stone, T.L. *Abraham Lincoln* (DK, 2005).

Swanson, James. *Chasing Lincoln's Killer* (Scholastic, 2009).

Index